Butterfly Notes

Story by
Dianne Wolfer

Illustrated by
Diana Platt

For Mrs Amphlett and Sophie

Butterfly Notes

Text: Diana Wolfer
Illustrator: Diana Platt
Editor: Kate McGough
Designer : Goanna Graphics (Vic) Pty Ltd
Typeset in platin
Reprint: Siew Han Ong

PM Plus Chapter Books
Emerald Level 26 Set B

Washed Away
Scamp
Boys Don't Dance!
The Saddest Dog
Lights in the Mine
Butterfly Notes

ISBN 978 0 17 009907 3
ISBN 978 0 17 009901 1 (set)

Cengage Learning Australia
Level 5 , 80 Dorcas Street
Southbank VIC 3006
Phone: 1300 790 853
Email: aust.nelsonprimary@cengage.com

For learning solutions, visit cengage.com.au

Printed in China by 1010 Printing International Ltd
24 23

Contents

Chapter One

Five Days to Go

Only five days until I play my violin in the school concert. Help!

I'll have to walk onto the school hall stage. Just me – Sarah Wood and my violin. It gives me butterflies thinking about it. Last year I performed with the other kids in Mrs Rondo's violin group. That was pretty scary, even though there were twelve of us. This year I'm doing a solo and I'm terrified!

After the solo, I'm in a duet with my friend, Stefan. He's really good, so I'm not too nervous about that. Then we'll also play four songs with the rest of our violin group. That should be okay because if you make a mistake, the others drown you out. It's the solo I'm worried about!

Mum says to ignore the butterflies and they'll go away, but I prefer Gran's idea for dealing with them.

Gran says that when the butterflies begin fluttering around my tummy, I should welcome them! Getting butterflies means that a chemical called adrenalin is charging through my blood and will make me play better. This sounds very weird to me, but Gran was a doctor before she retired, so I guess she knows.

And there's more…

After welcoming the butterflies, Gran suggests focusing on them.

"Let them fly from your tummy into your chest," she says. "Let them collect passion from your heart to take along your arm into your bow. Then imagine the butterflies changing into musical notes. Let them soar from your violin, off the stage and into the audience."

Yeah, sure! Gran tends to be a bit dramatic. She was also an actor in our town pantomime. I like her butterfly idea – really! It's just that when I get nervous, I can't think straight, so how can I imagine a butterfly migration?

Maybe Mum's advice is best after all. I cross another day off the calendar. Tomorrow it will be only…

Chapter Two

Four Days to Go

Tomorrow is my last lesson before the concert. Mrs Rondo gave me a list of things to practise. It's almost a kilometre long! Stefan's coming over today. We need to practise our duet. The doorbell rings. I bet it's him...

"Hi Stefan," I say.

"How's it going?" he smiles.

"Slowly! I'm not sure if I'm counting the beats properly."

"Let's put on the CD and see."

Stefan is only three months older than me, but he is much calmer. He's also really talented. There's something special about the way he plays his violin. It's as if he *feels* the music flowing from somewhere deep inside. I asked him about it once, but he blushed and changed the subject. He's very modest! We've been friends since pre-school. I'm lucky to have him as my duet partner.

Stefan's family live on the farm next door. I guess that's why Mrs Rondo suggested we perform together. It would have been hard to practise a duet with a kid from town. Stefan is way ahead of me in lessons. Sometimes I worry about that, and wonder if Stefan minds playing a piece that is so easy for him.

Stefan puts on the CD and we begin. He plays the harmony while I play the melody.

Stefan and I are like two threads running through the same piece of music. Sometimes it's his turn to be loud, and then it's mine. He nods to me as he finishes each bar.

Then it's time to practise *without* the CD. We take our violins out to the shed. It has good acoustics and there's a bench we use as our stage.

I pretend not to see my annoying twin brothers spying on us.